THE BIG BOOK OF BARBADOS FACTS

AN EDUCATIONAL COUNTRY TRAVEL PICTURE BOOK FOR KIDS ABOUT HISTORY, DESTINATION PLACES, ANIMALS AND MANY MORE

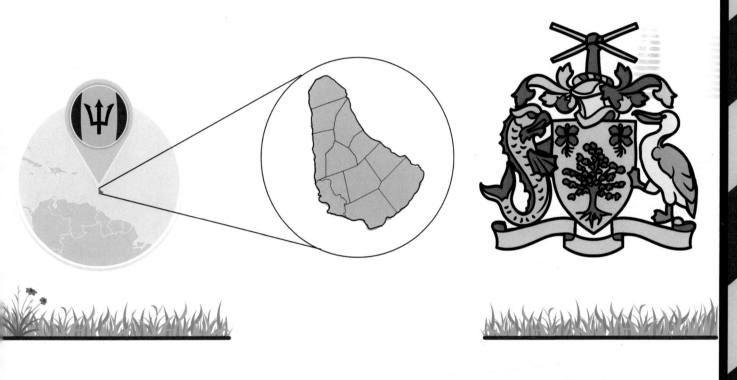

D1529979

Copyright @2023 James K. Mahi

Barbados is a small island country in the Caribbean Sea. It is the most eastern island in the Caribbean, which means it is the closest to Africa and Europe.

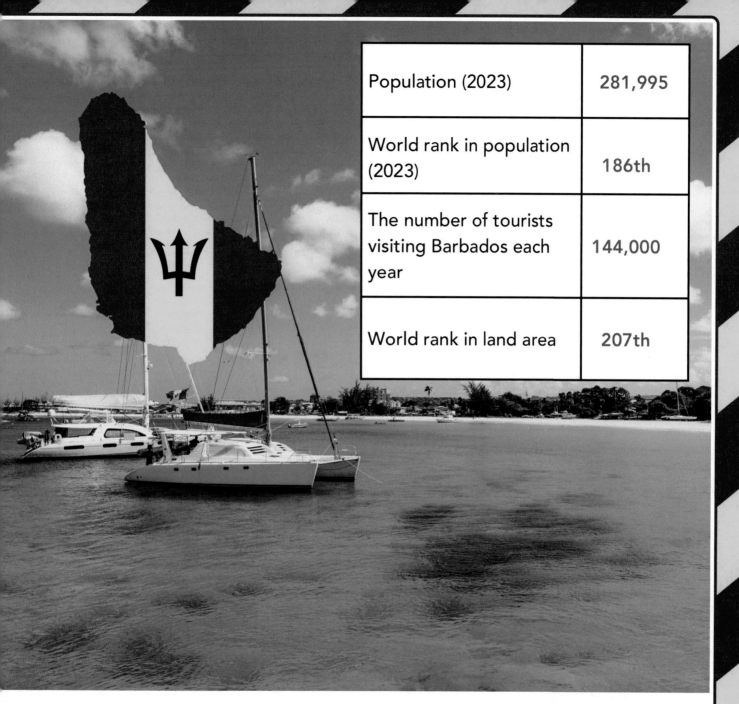

Population (2023)	281,995
World rank in population (2023)	186th
The number of tourists visiting Barbados each year	144,000
World rank in land area	207th

Barbados is shaped like a triangle. It is about 34 kilometers (21 miles) long and 24 kilometers (15 miles) wide. You can drive around the whole island in about three hours.

Barbados is mostly flat, but it has some hills in the center of the island. The highest point is Mount Hillaby, which is 340 meters (1,120 feet) above sea level.

The capital city of Barbados is Bridgetown.

Barbados is known for its beautiful white sandy beaches and crystal-clear waters.

Barbados is often called the "Land of Flying Fish" because flying fish are abundant in its waters.

Barbados is a popular destination for snorkeling and scuba diving due to its vibrant coral reefs.

The national currency of Barbados is the Barbadian dollar (BBD).

Barbados has a tropical climate with warm temperatures throughout the year.

Barbados was a British colony for over 300 years until it gained independence in 1966.

Barbados is known for its lively and colorful festivals, including Crop Over, which celebrates the sugar cane harvest.

Barbados is home to several species of sea turtles, **including the endangered Hawksbill and Leatherback turtles.**

The national dish of Barbados is cou-cou and flying fish. Cou-cou is a dish made from cornmeal and okra, and flying fish is a popular seafood delicacy in Barbados. The two dishes are often served together, and are considered to be the national dish of the island.

The Barbados Wildlife Reserve is a great place to see animals like green monkeys and peacocks in a natural setting.

The **Barbados Museum and Historical Society** is a great place to learn about the island's history and culture.

Cricket is the most popular sport in Barbados, and it has produced many international cricket stars.

The island is home to unique geological formations, such as limestone caves and underground lakes.

Barbados has a rich history of sugar cane production, and you can visit old sugar plantations to learn about this history.

Barbados has a vibrant arts and crafts scene, with many local artisans creating beautiful pottery, jewelry, and textiles.

The national flower of Barbados is the Pride of Barbados, known for its vibrant orange and red blossoms.

The island has a diverse marine life, making it a great spot for snorkeling and diving enthusiasts.

The Barbados is relatively flat, with the highest point being in the Scotland District.

The Chalky Mount Pottery is known for its distinctive pottery designs made using traditional techniques.

The Barbados main airport is Grantley Adams International Airport.

Barbados has a strong British influence, which is reflected in its architecture and traditions.

The island has a rich cultural heritage, with influences from Africa, Europe, and the Caribbean.

The Barbados National Trust preserves historic buildings and natural areas on the island.

Barbados is famous for its underground limestone caves, with Harrison's Cave being the most popular for tours.

Barbados has a unique tidal wave phenomenon known as the "Soup Bowl," which attracts surfers from around the world.

The island has a strong tradition of storytelling and folklore, with tales of mythical creatures like the "Jumbie."

Bridgetown's historic district is a UNESCO World Heritage Site.

Barbados is one of the top destinations for wedding and honeymoon tourism.

The island's economy relies heavily on tourism, sugar production, and offshore banking.

Barbados is home to several botanical gardens, including the Andromeda Botanic Gardens.

Barbados is a welcoming and friendly destination known for its warm hospitality and beautiful landscapes.

ENGLISH

The official language is English.

The island's national flag features a broken trident.

Mount Hillaby is the highest point in Barbados, reaching 1,120 feet (340 meters) above sea level.

Rihanna, the famous singer, was born in Barbados.

The currency of Barbados features a portrait of Queen Elizabeth II.

The legal drinking age in Barbados is 18 years old.

The national animal of Barbados is the mahi-mahi, also known as the common dolphinfish. It is a popular sport fish in Barbados, and is also commonly eaten.

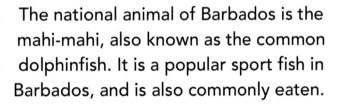

The national bird of Barbados is the brown pelican. The brown pelican is a large seabird that is commonly seen around the coast of Barbados. It is a popular symbol of the island, and is often featured on Barbadian currency and stamps.

Barbados is the birthplace of the grapefruit, which is a cross between a pomelo and an orange.

Barbados has the third oldest parliament in the Commonwealth, after the United Kingdom and Bermuda.

The first people to live in Barbados were the Arawak Indians, who arrived on the island from South America over 1,500 years ago.

Barbados is a great place to relax and have fun, with a variety of activities for kids of all ages, such as swimming, sunbathing, building sandcastles, playing beach volleyball, visiting the zoo, and exploring the underwater world.

TOP 10 TRAVEL TIPS FOR VISITING BARBADOS:

1. **Travel Documents:** Ensure your passport is valid for at least six months beyond your planned departure date. Some nationalities may require a visa, so check the entry requirements before you go.
2. **Weather:** Barbados has a tropical climate, so pack lightweight clothing, sunscreen, a hat, and insect repellent. Be prepared for occasional rain showers.
3. **Currency:** The currency in Barbados is the Barbadian dollar (BBD). It's a good idea to have some cash on hand for small purchases, but credit cards are widely accepted.
4. **Language:** English is the official language of Barbados, so you won't have any language barriers.
5. **Safety:** Barbados is generally safe for tourists, but exercise common-sense precautions. Avoid displaying valuables in public, be cautious at night, and lock your accommodations securely.
6. **Health Precautions:** Make sure you're up to date on routine vaccinations. It's also a good idea to drink bottled water and use sunscreen to protect against sunburn.
7. **Transportation:** Renting a car is a convenient way to explore the island, but remember to drive on the left side of the road. Alternatively, taxis and public buses are readily available.
8. **Local Cuisine:** Try the local food, including flying fish, cou-cou, and macaroni pie. Don't forget to sample some Barbadian rum, which is famous worldwide.
9. **Respect the Environment:** Barbados takes its natural beauty seriously. Respect the environment by not littering, avoiding touching or damaging coral reefs while snorkeling or diving, and following eco-friendly practices.
10. **Local Culture:** Barbados has a rich cultural heritage. Attend local festivals, visit historic sites, and interact with the friendly locals to get a taste of the island's unique culture.

Made in United States
Orlando, FL
05 March 2024

44440352R00024